I0447782

Mandala
Elegant Coloring Book

Copyright: Published in the United States by Tamara Loehr
Published December 2016
ISBN-13: 978-1541271753
ISBN-10: 1541271750

Thank you

www.ingramcontent.com/pod-product-compliance
Lightning Source LLC
Chambersburg PA
CBHW051946280526
45789CB00009B/3186
9781541271753